SPIRIT OF PLACE
TUSCANY

I look on those glorious hills, and turn to a map of Italy,
and long to lose myself in their depths, and to visit
every portion of Tuscany, every smaller town and secluded nook of
which is illustrious through historical association.

MARY SHELLEY, *RAMBLES IN GERMANY AND ITALY*, 1844

Arcade Publishing
New York

THE TUSCAN LANDSCAPE

Nobody looks at the view—except us—at the Euganean, bone white, this evening; then there's a ruddy red farm or two; and light islands swimming here and there in the sea of shadow—for it was very showery—then there are the black stripes of cypresses round the farm; like fur edges; and the poplars and the streams and the nightingales singing and sudden gusts of orange blossom; and white alabaster oxen with swinging chins—great flaps of white leather hanging under their noses—and infinite emptiness, loneliness, silence: never a new house, or a village; but only the vineyards and the olive trees, where they have always been. The hills go pale blue, washed very sharp and soft on the sky; hill after hill.

VIRGINIA WOOLF, *DIARY*, 15 MAY 1933

'THIS FAVOURED LAND . . .'

The impress of art – of industry, no less than that of a bounteous nature, is seen stamped upon the land unmistakeably. Fields, where not a weed is to be discerned; farms in which not one crooked or useless fence is visible, where the sower follows quick upon the reaper's track, and where the fresh turned-up sod is fast covered over by a bright carpet of verdure; where, from dawn till dusk, the labourer is seen plying spade or hoe indefatigably: all these things, seen in various parts of Tuscany, attest that the Tuscan peasant is far from being an ungrateful recipient of the bounties of Providence. As the traveller journeys in spring or summer through this favoured land, especially along the vale of the Arno, his onward course will be through scenes calculated to suggest the idea of a realised Arcadia. Far as the sight can reach on either side, farm after farm, for miles together, displays the same richness of produce, the same economy of space, the same garden-like degree of cultivation. Seen from a distance, the tile-roofed dwellings of the peasant, rising invariably at least two stories in height, though devoid of attraction as picturesque objects, seem to speak almost as strongly of comfort and prosperity as do the well-tilled fields, with their rich and varied produce, visible around them. Under the influences of the scene, bright are the pictures that fancy calls up before the traveller's eye, of the domestic life enjoyed by the Tuscan peasantry.

MABEL SHARMAN CRAWFORD, *LIFE IN TUSCANY*, 1859

TUSCAN TRANQUILLITY

Towards mid-day, we had surmounted the dreariest part of our journey, and began to perceive a milder landscape. The climate improved, as well as the prospect, and after a continual descent of several hours, we saw groves and villages in the dips of the hills, and met a string of mules and horses laden with fruit. I purchased some figs and peaches from this little caravan, and, spreading my repast upon a bank, basked in the sunshine, and gathered large spikes of lavender in full bloom.

Continuing our route, we bade adieu to the realms of poverty and bareness, and entered a cultivated vale, shaded by woody acclivities. Amongst these we wound along, the peasants singing upon the hills, and driving their cattle to springs by the road's side, near one of which we dined, in a patriarchal manner; and afterwards pursued our course through a grove of taper cypresses, waving with the cool gales of the evening. The heights were suffused with a ruddy glow, proceeding from the light pink clouds which floated on the horizon. No others were to be seen. All nature seemed in a happy, tranquil state; the herds penned in their folds, and every rustic going to repose. I shared the general calm, for the first time this many a tedious hour; and traversed the dale in peace, abandoned to flattering hopes and gay illusions. The full moon shone propitiously upon me, as I ascended a hill, and discovered Florence at a distance, surrounded with terraces and gardens, rising one above another.

WILLIAM BECKFORD, *DREAMS, WAKING THOUGHTS, AND INCIDENTS*, 1783

'FLOWERY TUSCANY'

Tuscany is especially flowery, being wetter than Sicily and more homely than the Roman hills. Tuscany manages to remain so remote, and secretly smiling to itself in its many sleeves. There are so many little deep valleys with streams that seem to go their own little way entirely, regardless of river and sea. There are thousands, millions of utterly secluded little nooks, though the land has been under cultivation these thousands of years. But the intensive culture of vine and olive and wheat, by the ceaseless industry of naked human hands and winter-shod feet, and slow-stepping, soft-eyed oxen does not devastate a country, does not denude it, does not lay it bare, does not uncover its nakedness, does not drive away either Pan or his children. The streams run and rattle over wild rocks of secret places, and murmur through blackthorn thickets where the nightingales sing all together, unruffled and undaunted.

D. H. LAWRENCE, 'FLOWERY TUSCANY', IN *NEW CRITERION*, OCT-DEC 1927

THE FLORENTINE COUNTRYSIDE

My driver pointed out a spot between the hills, on which lay a blue mist, and said 'Ecco Firenze!' I eagerly looked towards the place, and saw the round dome looming out of the mist before me, and the spacious wide valley in which the city is situated. My love of travel revived when at last Florence appeared. I looked at some willow trees (as I thought) beside the road, when the driver said, 'Buon olio', and then I saw that they were hanging full of olives. . .

About an hour before we arrived in Florence he said that the beautiful scenery was about to commence; and true it is that the fair land of Italy does first begin then. There are villas on every height, and decorated old walls, with sloping terraces of roses and aloes, flowers and grapes and olive leaves, the sharp points of cypresses, and the flat tops of pines, all sharply defined against the sky; then handsome square faces, busy life on the roads on every side, and at a distance in the valley, the blue city.

FELIX MENDELSSOHN, *LETTERS FROM ITALY AND SWITZERLAND*, 1865

'A City of Dreams . . .'

In the distant plain lay Florence, pink and gray and brown, with the rusty huge dome of the cathedral dominating its center like a captive balloon, and flanked on the right by the smaller bulb of the Medici chapel and on the left by the airy tower of the Palazzo Vecchio; all around the horizon was a billowy rim of lofty blue hills, snowed white with innumerable villas. After nine months of familiarity with this panorama I still think, as I thought in the beginning, that this is the fairest picture on our planet, the most enchanting to look upon, the most satisfying to the eye and the spirit. To see the sun sink down, drowned on his pink and purple and golden floods, and overwhelm Florence with tides of color that make all the sharp lines dim and faint and turn the solid city to a city of dreams, is a sight to stir the coldest nature and make a sympathetic one drunk with ecstasy.

MARK TWAIN, *THE AUTOBIOGRAPHY OF MARK TWAIN*, 1917

Where lies the secret spell of Florence? – a spell that strengthens, and does not fade with time?

It is a strange sweet subtle charm that makes those who love her at all, love her with a passionate, close-clinging faith in her as the fairest thing that men have ever builded where she lies amidst her lily-whitened meadows.

Perhaps it is because her story is so old, and her beauty is so young. . .

The past is so close to you in Florence. You touch it at every step. It is not the dead past that men bury and then forget. It is an unquenchable thing; beautiful and full of lustre, even in the tomb, like the gold from the sepulchres of the Etruscan kings that shines on the breast of some fair living woman, undimmed by the dust and the length of the ages.

OUIDA, *PASCAREL*, 1873

THE PONTE VECCHIO

Among the four old bridges that span the river, the Ponte Vecchio – that bridge which is covered with the shops of Jewellers and Goldsmiths – is a most enchanting feature in the scene. The space of one house, in the centre, being left open, the view beyond is shown as in a frame; and that precious glimpse of sky, and water, and rich buildings, shining so quietly among the huddled roofs and gables on the bridge, is exquisite. Above it, the Gallery of the Grand Duke crosses the river. It was built to connect the two Great Palaces by a secret passage; and it takes its jealous course among the streets and houses with true despotism: going where it lists, and spurning every obstacle away before it.

CHARLES DICKENS, *PICTURES FROM ITALY*, 1846

THE MEDICI VILLAS

It was also from Michelozzi's design and with his advice that Cosimo de' Medici made the palace of Cafaggiuolo in Mugello, giving it the form.of a fortress, with ditches surrounding it, and arranged the farms, ways, gardens, fountains in wooded groves, aviaries, and other requisites of a country house.

GIORGIO VASARI, *THE LIVES OF THE PAINTERS, SCULPTORS AND ARCHITECTS*, 1550

I went to Careggi, a most beautiful palace belonging to the same Cosimo [de' Medici], which I was able to inspect thoroughly; and it pleased me wonderfully; and I was no less impressed by the neatly kept gardens – which truly are too delightful to describe – than the worthy construction of the house itself, which has no less rooms and kitchens and halls and furnishings of every kind than those which are found in any of the splendid palaces in the city itself.

GALEAZZO MARIA SFORZA, LETTER, 1459

CARRARA

I went on foot three miles to Carara, through wooddy mountaines abounding with Chesse-nuts. The Towne is subject to the Prince of Masso, and is famous for the marble, which is much preferred before other, as well for the exceeding whitenes of some stones, as for the length of pillars and tables digged thence, which made it much esteemed at Rome in the time of the free state, and of the Empire; and by reason it lies neere the sea, the stones are more easily convaied to Rome, or els where. In one of the quarries called Pianella, I did see many stones digged out, which were as white as snow, and other quarries have veines of all colours; and they sell as much marble as an Ox will draw for twenty sols; but if it be carved there, the price is greater, according to the workemanship.

FYNES MORYSON, *AN ITINERARY*, 1617

LUCCA

Nothing could be more charming than the country between Lucca and Pistoia. If Pisa is dead Tuscany, Lucca is Tuscany still living and enjoying, desiring and intending. The town is a charming mixture of antique 'character' and modern inconsequence; and not only the town, but the country – the blooming romantic country which you admire from the famous promenade on the city-wall. The wall is of superbly solid and intensely 'toned' brickwork and of extraordinary breadth, and its summit, planted with goodly trees and swelling here and there into bastions and outworks and little open gardens, surrounds the city with a circular lounging-place of splendid dignity. This well-kept, shady, ivy-grown rampart reminded me of certain mossy corners of England; but it looks away to a prospect of more than English loveliness – a broad green plain where the summer yields a double crop of grain, and a circle of bright blue mountains speckled with high-hung convents and profiled castles and nestling villas, and traversed by valleys of a deeper and duskier blue.

HENRY JAMES, *ITALIAN HOURS*, 1909

SAN FREDIANO, LUCCA

The town is some thousand paces square; the unbroken rampart walk round may be a short three miles. There are upwards of twenty churches in that space, dating between the sixth and twelfth centuries; a ruined feudal palace and tower, unmatched except at Verona: the streets clean – cheerfully inhabited, yet quiet; nor desolate, even now. Two of the churches representing the perfectest phase of round-arched building in Europe, and one of them containing the loveliest Christian tomb in Italy. . .

The pure and severe arcades of finely proportioned columns at San Frediano, doing stern duty under vertical walls, as opposed to Gothic shafts with no end, and buttresses with no bearing struck me dumb with admiration and amazement; and then and there, on the instant, I began in the nave of San Frediano the course of architectural study which reduced under accurate law the vague enthusiasm of my childish taste.

JOHN RUSKIN, *PRAETERITA*, 1886-88 AND EPILOGUE TO 1883 EDITION OF *MODERN PAINTERS*

PISA

Let the reader imagine a small, white city, with a tower leaning at one end of it, trees on either side, and blue mountains for the background, and he may fancy he sees Pisa, as the traveller sees it in coming from Leghorn. Add to this, in summer-time, fields of corn on all sides, bordered with hedgerow trees, and the festoons of vines, of which he has so often read, hanging from tree to tree; and he may judge of the impression made upon an admirer of Italy, who is in Tuscany for the first time.

Leigh Hunt, Autobiography, 1850

Pisa is a fine old city that strikes you with the same veneration you would feel at the sight of an ancient temple which bears the marks of decay, without being absolutely dilapidated. The houses are well built, the streets open, straight, and well-paved; the shops well furnished; and the markets well supplied; there are some elegant palaces, designed by great masters. The churches are built with taste, and tolerably ornamented. There is a beautiful wharf of free-stone on each side of the Arno, which runs through the city, and three bridges thrown over it, of which that in the middle is of marble, a pretty piece of architecture: but the number of inhabitants is very inconsiderable; and this very circumstance gives it an air of majestic solitude which is far from being unpleasant to a man of a contemplative turn of mind. For my part, I cannot bear the tumult of a populous city; and the solitude that reigns in Pisa would with me be a strong motive to choose it as a place of residence.

Tobias Smollett, Travels through France and Italy, 1766

TUSCAN HARVEST

The vintage has begun here at San Gimignano. The equinox of autumn is over, the Pleiades have not yet set. On the roads the heavy farm carts drawn by two oxen are already lumbering from the vineyards to the *fattoria*, each fully loaded with tubs. It is a festal time. Under the still powerful sun a strange enchantment has fallen on the countryside; silvery wreaths of haze girdle the far blue hills and lie along the valleys. The vineyards, till now so silent and empty, are echoing with laughter and sprinkled with happy people; men and women, boys and girls and children too, from neighbouring *poderi*, have come to help the ingathering, not for pay or wages but in expectation of similar assistance in their turn. The *contadino* provides these helpers with bread, fruit and thin wine through the long day. In the golden weather, amid the general happiness and the beauty and profusion of the hanging clusters garlanded on high from maple to maple, one might almost fancy that Dionysus himself with Silenus and his rout are but out of sight in some shady dell where the stream still trickles in its dry bed in spite of the summer drought.

EDWARD HUTTON, *SIENA AND SOUTHERN TUSCANY*, 1955

SAN GIMIGNANO

I explored the battlements during one of those magic days in Tuscany when there appears to be no limit to one's vision. I looked north beyond the horizon to Florence, and south to Arezzo, while, only ten miles away, Siena sat enthroned upon her hills in knightly vigil, and so close she seemed in that spun air that I might have shot an arrow into her, or perhaps have tossed a gauntlet into the Campo, or maybe have shouted some taunt that would have been clearly heard and resented. Such thoughts are natural in the shadow of these towers.

H. V. MORTON, *A TRAVELLER IN ITALY*, 1964

S. Gimignano.

'I Discovered Siena . . .'

When I awoke that last morning the first thing I saw was a fantastic town of golden towers, surrounded by oak woods, lying some fifteen miles to the west. It was San Gimignano, that medieval parody of Manhattan, soaring, glittering and unbelievable.

Then, as I moved my head, suddenly I discovered Siena, hiding behind the bush. I had been waiting for my first sight of it, and I had somehow missed it in the twilight of yesterday. It stood far off, but clear, a proper city, rose-red and ringed by a great wall, with cathedral and palaces topping its trinity of hills and all the green country rising and breaking round it. It was a city compact as a carved Jerusalem held in the hand of a saint. And behind it hung a folded mountain, blue, like a curtain nailed against the sky.

LAURIE LEE, *I CAN'T STAY LONG*, 1975

There is nothing in the world quite like Siena; it is a medieval city that might be likened to a rare beast, with heart, arteries, tail, paws and teeth. Only the skeleton is left, intact, and it is enough to astound us.

BERNARD BERENSON, 1865-1959

THE PALIO

The approaches to Siena were jammed. From all over this part of Tuscany people were pouring into the town. . . As we crawled into the winding crowded streets the whole place vibrated with the noise and tingle of a fiesta in an effect at once delicate and dramatic, with its universal contrast of thrusting mobs, pink walls and blue sky. There is another constant contrast; black and white like a leit-motif of sun and shadow. You find both on the Piazza del Duomo in the striped white and basalt of the cathedral; and where the bricks of the old walls merge into pale stone with black outlines to each saracenic window-arch; and in the campanile that climbs up, course by course, in silver and jet; and on the terrace of the church, itself a draught-board dazzle, there were nuns in black and white and Domenicans in black and white; and over many doorways the final frequent assertion of the arms of the Bianchi and Neri – and all, remember, made doubly dazzling by the blazing sun and the flawless sky and the crowds surging along in high excitement. On any normal day one is almost surprised to come on any other colours than rose and black and white, or if not white a whitish yellow, soft as worn sea-shells, but on a special day like this day of the Palio when flags and banners in red and cerise and gold flare in every street Siena simply laughs with colour.

SEAN O'FAOLAIN, *A SUMMER IN ITALY*, 1949

ABOVE SIENA

Our rooms were in a tower. From the windows one looked across the brown tiled roofs to where, on its hill, stood the cathedral. A hundred feet below was the street, a narrow canyon between high walls, perennially sunless; the voices of the passers-by came up, reverberating, as out of a chasm. Down there they walked always in shadow; but in our tower we were the last to lose the sunlight. On the hot days it was cooler, no doubt, down in the street; but we at least had the winds. The waves of the air broke against our tower and flowed past it on either side. And at evening, when only the belfries and the domes and the highest roofs were still flushed by the declining sun, our windows were level with the flight of the swifts and swallows. Sunset after sunset all through the long summer, they wheeled and darted round our tower. There was always a swarm of them intricately manoeuvring just outside our window. They swerved this way and that, they dipped and rose, they checked their headlong flight with a flutter of their long pointed wings and turned about within their own length. Compact, smooth and tapering, they seemed the incarnation of airy speed.

ALDOUS HUXLEY, *ALONG THE ROAD*, 1925

'A PERFECTLY LONE HOUSE . . . '

Going over a rather bleak country (there had been nothing but vines until now: mere walking-sticks at that season of the year), stopped, as usual, between one and two hours in the middle of the day, to rest the horses; that being a part of every Vetturíno contract. We then went on again, through a region gradually becoming bleaker and wilder, until it became as bare and desolate as any Scottish moors. Soon after dark, we halted for the night, at the osteria of La Scala: a perfectly lone house, where the family were sitting round a great fire in the kitchen, raised on a stone platform three or four feet high, and big enough for the roasting of an ox. . . The waitress was a dramatic brigand's wife, and wore the same style of dress upon her head. The dogs barked like mad; the echoes returned the compliments bestowed upon them; there was not another house within twelve miles; and things had a dreary, and rather cut-throat, appearance.

CHARLES DICKENS, *PICTURES FROM ITALY*, 1846

A TUSCAN VILLA

This is a two-story house. It is not an old house – from an Italian standpoint, I mean. No doubt there has always been a nice dwelling on this eligible spot since a thousand years BC, but this present one is said to be only two hundred years old. Outside, it is a plain square building like a box and is painted a light yellow and has green window shutters. It stands in a commanding position on an artificial terrace of liberal dimensions which is walled around with strong masonry. From the walls the vineyards and olive orchards of the estate slant away toward the valley; the garden about the house is stocked with flowers and a convention of lemon bushes in great crockery tubs.

MARK TWAIN, *THE AUTOBIOGRAPHY OF MARK TWAIN*, 1917

CHIANTI

It may dream a little less, it may be less rumbustious now. But were the old ghosts to return, they would not feel out of place. Amerigo Vespucci could still slip back to his house at Montefioralle. Machiavelli could still play *tric-trac* at the inn across the road; Michelangelo and Galilei would still recognize their farms above Grignano. And Monna Lisa Gherardini, would still smile with secret pleasure at the view from Vignamaggio – which Leonardo drew on the feast of the Madonna delle Neve in 1473. . . Withdrawn and intact, and as beautiful as ever with its weathered contours, its villages and its farms, its churches and its hilltop castles, this is a land whose rhythms of change and growth have their roots in the deep pagan antiquity of the Etruscans or perhaps even earlier, maturing through generation after generation of dedicated toil. Here is a land whose equilibrium has been built up through an intimate link between man and the environment – whose charm and grace radiate over one with the same unconscious purity as a Sienese primitive.

RAYMOND FLOWER, *CHIANTI*, 1978

A Vineyard in Tuscany

I cannot help envying the Italians one charm that their country possesses: I mean her vines. Here the fields have rows of trees planted around them; and the trunks and branches of these trees are supporters of the vine, the greatest embellishment a country can possibly have. The vine is not at all the same thing here that it is in France. In France it is comparatively a humble thing. The French cut it down as nearly as we cut our currants, check its vigorous and aspiring shoots, and confine them to the height of a mere stake. It is not only to the palate, and to the sight on a general view of the country, that the vine here affords gratification. Each individual tree, or rows of trees, with the vines clambering up and hanging from the branches, is an object of admiration in itself. It is enough, without anything else, to characterise a whole country, and tells the stranger from the north that he has got into a quite new region.

JAMES COBBETT, *JOURNAL OF A TOUR IN ITALY*, 1830

THE FRUITS OF TUSCAN FIELDS

This is a marvellously fruitful country. Apart from the vines there are so many wild harvests. There are luscious blackberries everywhere, fat juicy sloes, Spanish chestnuts, juniper berries, mushrooms, hazelnuts, hawthorn berries. Earlier in the year there were wild strawberries, cherries and mulberries. There are many acorns too, beloved of the wild boar and also by the jays whose loud harsh call is often heard in the woods.

There are other nuts too – walnuts and almonds – and figs green and black; many of the old farmhouses have fig trees growing from crevices in the walls.

RAYMOND FLOWER, *CHIANTI*, 1978

W. Tyndale

A RURAL IDYLL

On my way to Arezzo I admired the Tuscan landscape which lay ahead, each hilltop holding a castle or a town. It was early in the morning, and as I went on I met country people on their way to market in Siena with eggs, vegetables, and crates of hens. I passed a young farmer standing upright in a cart, as poised as the charioteer of Delphi, while a lad walked at the head of two white oxen, whistling, singing, and from time to time speaking to them. With each step the great beasts swayed and nodded solemnly as if they understood the ox language he addressed to them, probably Etruscan, I thought.

The marriage of the Tuscan landscape to the New Testament has been the happiest of unions. The brown, silvery-grey countryside with its chestnut woods, its dark groves of cypress, its red-tiled farms, its outcrop of volcanic boulders, roofed by the blue Italian sky and palpitating to the sound of the cicada, is the most civilized rural scene on earth. It is embroidered everywhere by human living, and there is scarcely a hill, a stream, a grove of trees, without its story of God, of love or death.

H. V. MORTON, *A TRAVELLER IN ITALY*, 1964

TUSCAN WOMEN

The country women almost all wear pearl necklaces, and enormous ear-rings studded with pearls. These ornaments are a great matter of pride with the Tuscan peasantry. It is customary with the country men, when they get married, to make their brides a present of a necklace and ear-rings of pearl. The pearls are generally of inferior quality; but the quantity of them worn by one woman is so great, that the whole set often costs from twelve to fifteen English pounds. The people here do not appear to us so good-looking as those we saw about Genoa. Some of the country girls, however, are very handsome, and we noticed more pretty faces in passing through Campi than we have seen any where else at one time . . . they have fine brown complexions, glossy black hair parted over clear foreheads, and large eyes which are as mild in their expression as they are dark in their colour.

I have never seen a people so orderly as the Italians. They are now in the full enjoyment of the carnival; but you hear no brawling, see no drunkenness in the streets, and it would seem that nothing of this kind is to be witnessed here.

JAMES COBBETT, *JOURNAL OF A TOUR IN ITALY*, 1830

TUSCAN WHEATFIELDS

There comes the disrobing of the ground and its transfiguration through the wheat harvest. How often it has come upon me with surprise, this sense of relief, of a new world following on the steps of the reapers! The tree-trunks and roots, the vine-branches become suddenly visible, and the earth reveals itself, dry, pale, and almost disembodied in the sheen of stubble. And then all that much space, air, view gained! One misses, indeed, the sweetness rising from the cornfields at evening. But how far greater the deliciousness of their being open to breeze and light, of their long gleams and shadows, their rosiness on which the light lies golden, the shadows cut sharp and cool. And then the freedom of walking over the stubble, of seeing the other crops, young maize and beans and sorghum, noting for the first time the little green apples on the trees that bend over, and the grapes, still minute, but quite shapely. One watches the oxen ploughing once more between the vine-garlands in the wonderfully sweet twilights, when the sawing of the cicalas meets for a moment the far gentler, but shriller, note of the crickets; the two voices of the Italian summer, so oddly suited, one to the blazing, relentless day, the other to the gentle and friendly night.

VERNON LEE, *THE TOWER OF MIRRORS*, 1914

Valombrossa

We could not resist the temptation of visiting Valombrossa. It is true this is not the season for excursions, autumn being too far advanced; but a fine day gave us promise, we hoped, for the same on the morrow: so we hired a *vettura* and set out.

The road skirts the river, and winds up the Valdarno, the slopes of whose inclosing hills are thickly studded with country seats. It was a showery day; but the sun shone at intervals, and brightened the stream and mountain sides. The road is new and good. At about one o'clock we reached a small town where a cattle fair was going on. After some delay, however, we got ponies and a guide, and proceeded. We now fell upon a true mountain path, winding up the hill beside a brawling torrent; the crags rose high above, and the branches of noble forest-trees were spread over our path – truly they were in the sear and yellow leaf; but the place was the more consonant with Milton's verse:

Thick as autumnal leaves that strow the brooks
In Valombrossa, where th'Etrurian shades
High over-arched embower.

As we climbed higher, a shower of sleet came on, and we arrived wet through at the Convent. . . The grassy plain, or platform, before the Convent is at the head of a huge gully or ravine, which slopes down towards the valley of the Arno. A mist hung over the scene; but in summer-time it must be – what it is named – Paradise.

MARY SHELLEY, *RAMBLES IN GERMANY AND ITALY*, 1844

ACKNOWLEDGEMENTS

PICTURE CREDITS

Front cover: *The Duomo, Florence, from the Mozzi Gardens*, Henry R. Newman (Sotheby's)
Back cover: *An Italian Fruit Stall*, Walter Tyndale (Fine Art Photographic Library/Chris Beetles Ltd)
Frontispiece: *Florence*, Henry Tonks (Bridgeman Art Library /Victoria & Albert Museum)
3: *Dawn, San Gimignano*, Jan Traylen (Patrick Eagar)
5: *Study of a Peasant*, A. Faldi (Scala, Florence)
7: *A Roadside Shrine on the Outskirts of Florence*, Karl Marko (Fine Art Photographic Library)
9: *Italian Monastery Garden*, Dennis Stock (Magnum)
11. *Florence*, Samuel Palmer (Bridgeman/V&A Museum)
13: *The Duomo, Florence, from the Mozzi Gardens*, Henry R. Newman (Sotheby's)
15: *The Duomo, Florence*, John Ross (Susan Griggs Agency)
16: *Ponte Vecchio, Florence*, John Sims
17: *Ponte Vecchio, Florence*, William Holman Hunt (Bridgeman/V&A Museum)
18: *Villa Caffagiolo*, Ted Spiegel (Susan Griggs Agency)
19: *Villa Carregi*, Ted Spiegel (Susan Griggs Agency)
21: *Carrara*, Paolo Koch (Vision International)
23: *On the Walls, Lucca*, Henry Herbert Bulman (Bridgeman/V&A Museum)
25: *Interior of San Frediano, Lucca*, John Ruskin (Manchester City Art Gallery)
27: *Pisa*, John Sims
29: *Vineyards in Chianti*, John Sims
30: *San Gimignano*, Brian Harris (Impact Photos)
31: *San Gimignano*, John Fulleylove (Bridgeman/V&A Museum)
33: *Siena*, John Sims
35: *The Cathedral, Siena*, Richard Henry Wright (Bridgeman/V&A)

37: *Siena* (Tony Stone Wordwide)
39: *'Le Crete'*, John Sims
41: *An Italian Villa*, Walter Tyndale (Chris Beetles Ltd)
43: *Chianti*, John Sims
45: *A Vineyard in Tuscany*, Giovanni Costa (Fine Art Photographic)
47: *An Italian Fruit Stall*, Walter Tyndale (Fine Art Photographic/Chris Beetles Ltd)
49: *Rural Scene near San Gimignano*, Henri Cartier-Bresson (Magnum/John Hillelson Agency)
51: *Returning from the Village Fête*, Aurelio Tiratelli (Bridgeman/Gavin Graham Gallery)
53: *Wheatfield near Volterra*, Charlie Waite (Landscape Only)
55: *Valombrossa*, William B. Spence (Fine Art Photographic)

TEXT CREDITS

Text extracts from the following sources are reprinted with the kind permission of the publishers and copyright holders stated. Should any copyright holder have been inadvertently omitted they should apply to the publishers who will be pleased to credit them in full in any subsequent editions.

2: Virginia Woolf, *A Writer's Diary* (Hogarth Press, 1953) Courtesy of The Estate of Virginia Woolf and The Hogarth Press/Harcourt Brace Jovanovich; 28: Edward Hutton, *Siena & Southern Tuscany* (Methuen, 1955); 30, 48: H. V. Morton, *A Traveller in Italy* (Methuen, 1964); 32: Laurie Lee, *I Can't Stay Long* (Andre Deutsch, 1975); 34: Sean O'Faolain, *A Summer in Italy* (Eyre & Spottiswoode, 1949); 36: Aldous Huxley, *Along the Road* (Chatto & Windus, 1925) Courtesy of Mrs Laura Huxley and Chatto & Windus/Harper & Row; 42, 46: Raymond Flower, *Chianti* (Croom Helm, 1978).

Published in the United States by Arcade Publishing, Inc.,
a Little, Brown company.

Library of Congress Cataloging-in-Publication Data is available.

ISBN 1-55970-008-4
First American Edition

Conceived, edited and designed by Russell Ash and Bernard Higton
Printed and bound in Spain by Cayfosa, Barcelona

10 9 8 7 6 5 4 3 2 1